New & Selected Poems

Acknowledgements

The poems in the first part of this book, to page 66, are reprinted from *Endorphin Angels* (Smith|Doorstop, 2001)

Thanks are due to the following publications, where several of the previously uncollected poems first appeared: *The North*, *Poetry Daily website*, *Poetry London*, *Poetry Review*, *The Rialto*.

New and Selected Poems
Dennis Casling
edited by Julia Copus and Annie Freud

smith|doorstop

Published 2018 by
Smith|Doorstop Books
The Poetry Business
Campo Houses
54 Campo Lane
Sheffield S1 2EG
www.poetrybusiness.co.uk

Copyright © The estate of Dennis Casling 2018

ISBN 978-1-910367-92-6

The estate of Dennis Casling hereby asserts his moral right to be identified as the author of this book.

British Library Cataloguing-in-Publication Data.
A catalogue record for this book is available from the British Library.

Typeset by Utter
Printed and bound by CPI Group (UK) Ltd, Croydon, CR0 4YY
Cover image: Michele Casling Powell
Author photo: Michele Casling Powell

Smith|Doorstop is a member of Inpress, www.inpressbooks.co.uk. Distributed by NBN International, Airport Business Centre, 10 Thornbury Road Plymouth PL 6 7PP.

The Poetry Business receives financial support from Arts Council England

Contents

11	Initiation
13	In the Farmyard
14	Children's Voices at Breakfast
15	Lifting
16	Family
17	Blue
18	The Cabbage Cutter
19	The Moon and the Fat Man
20	When I Died
21	Where Does the Dark Go?
22	What the Blind Man Sees
23	Fish
25	Church Window
26	Reflection in a Photograph
28	The Unicorn
29	Stag's Skull
30	The Artist Walks to Work
31	Bonnard: The Open Window
32	The Anatomy Lesson
33	Mandelstam
34	Shostakovitch
35	The Shape of Things
36	Sisyphus
37	Signs
38	Viola Weather
39	Morning
40	Absence
41	The Convenience of Bridges

43	In the Imperial War Museum
45	Arms
46	Removals
47	Holiday
48	Fear
49	Shells and Butterflies
50	Eurydice
51	Hackenback's Limp
53	Nag's Head, Cape Hateras
54	Montana de Oro Bay
55	Disney World
56	The Plan
57	Scrap
58	The Garden of Eden
59	Ark of the Covenant
60	Jacob's Ladder
61	Holding On
63	Cow
64	The Train
65	A Dream of Football
66	Dissolution
67	The Laugh
68	The Stranger
69	Scrape
70	Epithalamion
72	Happy Families
73	Self Portrait with House
74	Sound
76	The Disappearance of the Sock
77	Daughter

78	Shaving the Fool
80	Tally
81	Wardrobe
82	Winging It
83	The Poet Reclining
84	This Poem
85	Guilty
86	The Fiery Lake
87	The Rule
88	Straw Hats and Parasols
89	Hedda Gabler
90	What to Do?
91	The Poet in the Rain
92	Wash, O God, Our Sons and Daughters
93	Man with a Suitcase
94	House Hunting
95	The Solid Body
96	Return
97	The Iceman
98	Self Portrait with Saxon Helmet
99	Winter Rain
100	Anatomy of a Winter Evening
101	Snail
102	Rapunzel
104	The Plunge
105	Man in a Box
106	The Wish
107	Uses of a Goatherd
108	Midwinter
109	Love Poem

110	The Unexpected
112	Widow
113	Indian Summer
114	Heart
115	A Rainy Day
116	Against Time
117	Dialysis
118	The Resurrection of the Body
119	The End

Initiation

Egg

I am sitting in the dark. I am female.
I am about to roll. With my sisters I am waiting.
We are sitting in water, knocking softly against each other
like pebbles on a shore. The tumult reaches us
through glass, though glass and water and sisterhood
are not yet arrived. It is the faintest movements in air,
thistledown, fairy wings, a dragon fly pulse.
We put down our mirrors that sit inside us.
Over our white faces we pull on the masks of gods.
We look disinterested. The air hums.
Our roundness smiles. Far off a thrashing of tails.

Sperm

In bathrooms and bedrooms all over suburbia
we gaze into mirrors. We are beside ourselves.
Waxing our hair and flexing our muscles,
we stare into the vacancy that is our eyes.
The sun sets like an oil slick. At one precise moment
all the street lights go on. We leave our front doors.
We will give of our best. One of us tonight
is the lucky one. Dark and forceful,
he won't take no for an answer. Eyes downcast,
she will swoon in her whiteness,
waiting for her bubble to burst.

Foetus

Lord of the startled heartbeat, naked Buddha.
Slumped in the juice of distraction. Thumb in mouth.
Lungs like deflated balloons. No questions asked.
Monotonous throbbing of pulses. Tadpole.
Nerves crawling through the body like spiders.
Your mother's expectant moon snagged in the branches.
Beyond the edges of the dark there is more dark.
There is the world of the unexpected.
Gravity will tip you suddenly upside down.
Before you know it, your perfect self
will slide slowly, effortlessly from you
like splinters of glass from a shattered mirror.
We will watch helplessly our broken reflections
in the pieces, unable to put them back.

In the Farmyard

Travelling the cow's backbone from rump to shoulder –
a bamboo ridge pole on rocky mounds;
slung under
a furry globe, the finger
tracing down latitudes of winter coat,
soft as a baby's hair;
the flat milk sack warm on the hand,
like a child's fever.
Four rubbery teats angled like chair legs;
pulling down melodies of milk
into a tin bucket.

Crossing the cobbled yard, laced
with flailed grains of oat and barley,
the cold rings in the ears, like a blacksmith's hammer,
freezing history into the senses. The midnight blue sow, pink saddled,
slumps on her side, exhausted, as though ridden there,
her eyes half closed with the ecstasy of sucking mouths.
One piglet detaches herself, navigates
the southern tip of trotter, the gulf of throat,
across the inlet of the mouth into the warm storm
of nostril, putting in, snuffling, at the ears,
before releasing herself
in a parabola of discovery,
reinventing the passage of her life.

My little daughter in her mother's arms
laughs like a chicken, asks,
'Are they eating her?'

Yes, they are eating her.

Children's Voices at Breakfast

The boy has silver hair, blue eyes and freckles.
He wears a New York Yankees baseball cap.
He draws cartoons of men with muscles like mountains.
He watches TV and thinks we go on and on for ever,
as he says, till we land up in heaven or hell.

The girl listens with her dark eyes.
The tea's brown tongue is licking out the cup,
she says, as if to nobody.

When you fold your memories in the map
of all the moments you have ever had,
the cup is stillness on your lips.
The words of children never counted much.
We shut them out. Yet it's for you alone
they give their silence up, to show you
something you will never have again.

Lifting

I lift my son, warm from his bed.
He is tall now, half my length,
and heavy in my arms.
Somnolent on tiptoe, he staggers,
penis erect, pisses. We listen to the sound
of water on water. He drops his head.

Back in my arms he slumps asleep.
He fits his body to my body.
I am a walking bed.
He could be comfortable in the branches of a tree.
He lifts his head and manages
three words, Where, where, where?
Even in sleep he wants his mother.

In his bed he whispers me, goodnight,
and I return to kiss him,
but he is already gone.

Down the landing his baby sister wakes.
I go to her more willing than a lover,
more in demand. She roots for food,
her arm around my neck. I take her to her mother.

Family

No sun distils a midday mist hanging
from beech to beech. It spins a film of moisture
on our faces, that keeps us disengaged.
We sink in the accumulated scent of leaves.

In a fire's half light in the drawing room
eyes gleam in lazy conversation. Children
moon from one distraction to another.
The eight month baby in my lap looks
from family to flame, his eyes cold blue
and fascinated. Grasping the air up
like a curtain. His brain is brimmed with language.

So, in ember light in the evening we play
charades, and I get *Laughter in the Dark*.
I act the last word first.

Blue

Three blue bottles on a windowsill,
sunlight white on the rim, her velvet dress
thrown on the bed – a green snake skin sloughed off.
Everything bathed in elemental light.
Everything changed, washed off. The bed turned back.
The man who lowed and grunted like the beasts
and saw himself ridiculously a god –
she sees him in her telescope
the wrong way round. He's miniscule as moons.
Silk green lizards run up her body,
flick-flicking their tongues in the directions of her mouth.
Fat bodied grasshoppers drift across her eye line.
A skeletal bird pecks at her face.
Sometimes her anger is a box for crying in,
unfurling on a ribbon of song snatches
like clothes on a washing line –
'soft bellied love', 'a slippery beauty'.
It itches and scratches her like brambles.
The delicate porcelain water jug
placated her, poisons leaching from her
down a stream that ends at these three bottles,
blue as blue against a varied sky.
The three blue poison bottles emptied of everything
but sunlight slanting on the window sill.

The Cabbage Cutter

Late afternoon of summer,
the thick, still air choked with remote voices.
Wood doves cooing, amorous feathered gods.
A man in shirt sleeves slams the door of a beat up car.
Coming from work, his tie undone. He saunters,
glances back at the road he's come along. Into the shop.

Propelled by his entrance, the mechanics of motion,
another man leaves by the back door. A grey-haired man
in heavy boots and shorts – brown legs, dark brown knees.
He walks down rows of black green savoys.
Astride one, he lobs off the firm fresh head
with a kitchen knife. The cabbage squeals.
The first man stands on the front porch, oblivious,
hands in pockets, listening. He straightens up
with the other man's return. They exchange a few words.
He carries the head triumphantly, tosses it on the back seat.

Dust rises. The hedgerow snatches at it.
The dead returned as birds settles their wings.
There is a murmuring in the air,
as if something undreamed of has finally happened.

The Moon and the Fat Man

Under a full moon wind ruffles grass tussocks.
New lambs frantically seeking on moonlit fells.
Irregular hills jag the dark skyline.

Across from here the fat man fills the lighted window,
sits sideways at table, eating in dungarees.
By day he grows potatoes in neat rows –
green tops muddied, hanging for the water
he brings in buckets. Fat and thoughtful in dungarees.
Lifted up here, all there is to do is eat them.

How far the lambs' cries carry on the wind.
The fat man cocks his ear, stops chewing,
lays down his fork beside his plate,
his face three quarter silhouette.
How close the moon. How deep the wet roots.

When I Died

When I died, it was a beginning.
My body was washed down by a woman
with rubber gloves on her elegant fingers.
I watched her remotely. She hesitated
over my penis. The air around me smiled.
I was free, my heart resting at last.
My sphincters took holiday. I flew out
somewhere, last minute, fast as light.

My dog moped in the basket. My wife awake
all night, the dark full of voices.
I called the huge distances. My children heard
and turned their pale faces to the window.
The wind threw handfuls of rain at the glass.
Year on year the trees whispered away their leaves.

Where Does the Dark Go?

Darkness brings everything closer, hand in glove,
a word in the ear. Horizons disappear.
Distant trains scissor off the edge of town,
run their cold wheels along your cheek bone.

Lovers push darkness back into each other,
though it seeps out through half closed eyes.
It rolls around the throat like thunder,
the tongue a swollen corpse in a sacred river.
Exhausted, they fall back into it and drown.

On clear, still nights in winter snow turns blue,
and the cock crow breaks off pieces in silence.
You will see fires flare in the charcoal sky.

When dawn comes, the dark is taken down,
and folded into thick green woods, where foxes
gnaw at it all day, mistaking it for carrion.

What the Blind Man Sees

What is this space? Nothing? Emptied of light,
the night still has its stars, or darker clouds.
Visited by angels, angelic forms
of light, high mountains of illumination,
but inside the head. Not the last white light of dying,
but diffuse glimmer of palpitating wings.

Endorphin angels? I've seen them on mountains.
In the valley where a ribbon of white water
tumbles into a green pool, liquid lines of sheep
flowing across fells. High above them, seraphic bodies
as far as the eye can see, filling the imagined sky,
taking over from this darkness, emptied of light.

Fish

We drove into the Welsh hills above Llandovery –
lines of headstones propped against the chapel walls,
as if workmen were digging up the past.

We camped in a triangle of grass between road and river.
From tent to car we tied a rope that guided me,
guided my first footsteps into the dark.
You were learning to be a blind man's wife,
to read tombstone names to me in my darkness.

In those days the least excursion took me hours,
summoning the courage from somewhere to stumble and be stared at.

On the second morning you were tidying the ground,
and must have from the corner of your eye caught
the bright leap of the fish. I heard it –
and saw it too in my mind's eye, upright,
arching its iridescent back, the eye fixed
blindly on the direction it was taking.
We shared what we had seen. My eye as valid as yours.
Later you coaxed me naked into a deep pool,
where the river had piled up boulders and dammed itself,
feeling with my feet for rock holds in the clear water, down
and all the way under. My eyes ached with cold.
I leaped back, clearing my shoulders with a whoop.

Later, you, pregnant, lying on your side,
I loved the touch of your tightening skin, breasts bulging with milk,
your heavy belly flattened on the ground.
Round and round my hands went. Suddenly the baby kicked
and rose like a fish in a river. I almost caught him.
He must have hung there in the amniotic fluid
like a fish hovering against the flow, listening,

waiting and waiting on heart beat, hearing our distant voices.
When he came out of you, he mewed like a cat,
and someone placed him in my arms, wrapped in paper.
I stared blindly into the crack he made in time.
Someone turned of a tap. Now at a bus stop
he is a moon to a cluster on girls,
a young bull with school bag hunched against the rain.

You and I in a quiet time sit wondering.
The clock from the Llandovery farmhouse hangs
on the wall and booms the hours away.
The room fills with silence as the river fills endlessly,
endlessly cleaning itself, waiting for fish to jump.

Church Window
A blind man looks at a photograph

Your hand on mine moves from side to side
across the photograph. In one corner
hang cobwebs, sagging under the unseen
weight of age. Our hands, like coupling spiders,
examining the candid rectangle
of church window. A lengthened cross divides
panes of clear glass. Pain peels from the recess,
where dead carnations in a stone vase turn
to dust.

This broken moment where we focus
in hand and eye all our expectation.
Beyond the rectangle, beyond the cross,
beyond the desiccating, flaking stone,
my finger traces suddenly a crest
of hill descending like your collar bone.

Reflection in a Photograph

You look at me – a silver nitrate ghost
floating in the alchemy of words.
You gaze back down the road you have come along,
back towards that little, ordinary, cocky girl,
propped there in party dress before the camera.
Born, as they said, half bird, your wings clipped
painfully in plastic, itched and comforted
by women, enrolled into mythologies
of wings and preciousness and incompletenesses
by storytellers we never asked to speak.
Afraid to let you fly, they taught you how to fall.
Never asked to be born, we were always here,
watching and wondering and being gawped at.
Because I couldn't see, they couldn't see me.

You are my mirror. You give me back my body
in the space between us, made of voice and emptiness,
of difference and commonality.
I am lost and found in your reflection.

What are we waiting for – anybody, nobody?
Always and already, we start from here.
We were told by ghost voices long ago,
there was one body, one mind, one way of being whole.
I was that anxious boy wondering if it was true.
And somewhere on that sudden road from childhood,
where mouths dropped open when we dared to pass,
I learned we live in many bodies – breath body,
breast body, tongue, mouth, cunt body, holy body, dream body.
But some body chose this body to carve
their negligence and nightmares on.

We learned to be lonely at heart, and from the heart
emerging slowly, little by little,
leg, foot, breast, thigh, eyes, voice – a hand opening
finger by finger, palm up, offering what we had to give.
No need to call the tune. We were always the tune.

How beautiful, described to me, your nakedness,
however wrapped in perspex fantasy.
Your wholeness makes me whole.
Not winged but grounded womanhood, whose gaze
must shame us out of myths of imperfection.
We have come a long way, and are here now,
burning, crowned in flame.
No weather in the world can blow us down.

The Unicorn
After Rainer Maria Rilke

This is the one of uncertain existence
who lingered timidly in Eden,
and never wandered out along their path of knowledge;
yet they invested her in flesh –
upright, silk necked, loose flanked,
and, caught in her shimmering gaze, they loved her.

Desire howled for her,
when they glimpsed her on the edge of battle,
Gideon's angel, nonchalant under the oak;
or, reflected in the priest's bright chalice
lifted in smoking candle light;
or, when other, impatient angel's creaked their wings
above them, sweat on their side curls, she entered
their emptiness, raising her gentle head,
hesitant on the threshold of existence.

They fed her not on grain,
but on the possibility of being,
and in itself this gave her such pure strength,
she grew miraculously a horn,
a single horn, out of her forehead.

She carried her own soft whiteness willingly to them,
and, fixed in their silvered mirror, walked
innocently into it,
moving silkily, ambiguously deep inside.

Stag's Skull

Turn the photo round – the angle falsifies:
out of a shaded cranny an owl's head
watches us. Round again – the old stag's skull,
big as a rock, the fault line visible.
Antlers sawn off, cropped to the bone,
that must have swelled and steepled like a tree.
He'd lock them knocking in a rutting drive,
or shake them, grunting hugely at the moon.

Mute now, he's lit dramatically for you
to trigger off your death defying shots,
studioed and studied for the sake of art –
a form with abstract possibilities:
though captive, penitent, cut down to size,
still menacing, still poised, still imminent.

The Artist Walks to Work

Along this simple avenue of trees
the painter, shirt and easel, hat and shadow,
strides to work. His nonchalant straw hat,
his devil-may-care trousers. The distant hills
give up their blueness, the corn its yellow.

I walk this white imagined road, dust on my shoes,
dreaming the artist under artless cypresses.
Sit in purple fields at dusk among almond shells.

I trace the road to Mont Saint Victoire –
the map on the studio wall had shown it,
under gigantic, shivering plane trees.
There is no visionary mountain. I look everywhere.
All I find is a dry well and corn stubble.

Late in the indigo evening I meet the artist,
those inconsolable eyes, on the undiscoverable road.

Bonnard: The Open Window

In this room you sleep the sleep of the dead,
your old head on blue canvas.
Dreams steal to you in cat silence.

The window opens on greeness
like a new thought. The tree touches
the translucent blue of vast distances.

A blue vase is a handful of sky:
the shutters and the dark blind a camera.
The cat moves her head ambiguously.

This blue, this wide, infinite air
holds the window open one long moment,
while you sleep the sleep that fills the room.

The Anatomy Lesson

In the underground car park three black men take the keys.
Two don't speak English. They offer to wash the car.
In the cave mouth you look at the opulent arch
of the bird cage Opera House. Heads down in the rain,
still smiling, ears ringing with the German syllables
of Mozart. The corporate clients make their way
to where flunkies hold the car door open
for a quick getaway. In a tenement block
a black woman carries washing in a basket
to the launderette. BMWs cruise past with smoked windows.

Men in black tail coats frozen in candle light
around the dissecting table frown with authority.
The surgeon peels back the layers of the dead woman.
They have come from a dinner party, the opera, the theatre.
In the limelight of science they stare at the mise-en-scéne
of the woman's open womb. They are expecting the moon,
but the moon has taken herself away behind clouds.
Instead one has arranged a foetus in a jar
with beads. White as a pickled egg. A pickled moon.
Down the corridor we watch the simulated movements
of hysterics. Real leather ovary compressors.
A padded jacket keeps the body straight.

I am a blind man. A man living on the streets asks
if we are lost. For a few pennies he can show us.
Show us what? I shrug my shoulders. What is there to see?

Mandelstam

> *'Nobody has said they actually saw Osip dead. Nobody claims to have washed the body or put it in the grave. I can be certain of only one thing, that somewhere Osip's suffering ended in death.'*

After the rocking horse headlamps of the car,
the dream of forests, the misty river crossing,
the stammering internment of the sun,
the upstart poet wakes and watches. His senses
stick to nothing, the face framed in the window,
fixed, discharged, disintegrating, open,
reiterating the rhythm of the journey,
the space around him crowded with betrayal:
a hero from nowhere rattling into exile
under the hard, articulate, calm, bright stars.
He knows the worm, that winters in the Veronesh hills,
will plough its bloodless furrow in his brain.

Here at the co-ordinates of breathlessness and death
they take from him his coat, his shirt, his boots.
He gives them back the black words from his throat.
They stand around frozen to what he knows.

She holds the emptiness in her crooked arm.
Dreams wake her. She wraps herself in hope.
She writes, 'My beloved, far-away sweetheart,
I have no words to write this letter to you;
I send it into an empty space.
It is me, Nadya: where are you?'

He takes the hills, the sky,
the kiss of separation,
and puts them on for clothes.
He shakes his head,
and from it fall diamonds

Shostakovitch

Boldly
he seeks
from the rostrum
the face of the ruling clique.
His tight mouth refuses their nostrum.
His black eyes
speak.

In front of the smiling players
he bows like a skittery horse,
his eyebrows arched in question marks
over the wild applause.

His questions hang like rags on wire,
like skin on bone,
like souls on fire.

Slowly
he searches the faces
that burn in the edge of light.
Amazement
washes him clean as a corpse.
His cheek is ashen white.

He tangles himself in dilemma,
in the minutes and hours of doubt.
Wrapped like a drowning swimmer in water,
he is snagged like a hook in a trout.
They love him.
They won't let him out.

The Shape of Things

Euclid saw it. It hung there
for a moment in front of him,
came and went. Its sides were sheer.
A kite in the cerebral air.
Euclid tugged on the string. The shape moved.
He saw the lines of its sides, its angles, its corners.
Drew it in sand. Rubbed it out with his foot.
Started again. Over and over.
The memory of it stuck to his toes.
Entered the tips of his fingers.
He has never seen anything so straight and true.
Always his shapes had been breasts or moonlight,
softly rounded, somewhere to sleep in,
to collide with. But this shape was distant.
In the head, away from the body.
It thrilled him with its absolute edges.
Euclid saw it hovering before him –
the ghost of an idea.

Sisyphus

Not one for myths, Sisyphus. Carry on like this,
he'll have himself in history. Breathes heavy,
mouth full of stone-dust. You'd think he'd get it
second time around, third, fifth, ad infinitum.
Maybe, if he pushes long and hard enough,
this boulder takes off and walks the rest itself.
He'd stand there sweating, wondering what he'd done.

You might suppose Newton would be wise to it,
first time he dropped his trousers by mistake.
He wasn't thinking straight, eyes full of stars,
other fish to fry. What did he do?
Double locked them with a belt or two.

It seems the moment has to bring itself to being.
When questions hit you on the head. Now gravity's
the order of the day. Pushing against it's the thing.

Night falls. Man falls. Walls come tumbling down.
One law to govern everything? Words fall
between us. We never seem to learn,
or learn too late, as rocks fly past our ears,
we must imagine Sisyphus is happy.

Signs

When Jacques Derrida came, we went to hear,
aimless in inarticulate pursuit
of wisdom, dapper in its tie and suit,
that made the ground beneath us disappear,
a sense of disconnection taking root.

My half deaf friend stood up to make a point.
Derrida didn't understand his drift,
and, seeking signs, began to search his face.
They stood in limbo like the desert saints.
I watched Derrida knot his tie and lift
one hand, as if delivering a grace.

Viola Weather

This is viola weather. Wakes the house
to haunting. Wind punches windows. Doors settle.
A gangling dog slumps thumping on the floor.
Stranded in armchairs, wind waves lapping
round the walls. Rain squalls chaotic grains.
I am nerve ends. Mister Stevens rainy man.

Daydream – a dialogue with time. The old way out.
One bound and he was free. No trains going my way
on empty, soot flaked stations. Greatcoated,
pockets stuffed with paperbacks, twenty something,
all coat and elbows, hunched over coffee cups.
Aluminium doors swoons shut after a passenger.
I'm reading *Herzog*. I remember the name!
I lasso the moment from the comfort of middle age,
books kept me warm. I was blanketed in print.
Cafeteria staff in green aprons.
Was that the colour? Did coffee taste like that?
The memories call out from that dangerous moment,
the cigarette gesture, look avoiding looks,
steam trains hissing on other empty platforms,
a book's title, waiting. Did I ever leave?
A train whistle out of the station tunnel –
the long, slow, steady, low, held note of a viola.

Morning

I am
a stranger stepping from a train,
dragging the baggage of night behind him,
flat footed
on the platform, waiting for someone,
anyone, to receive him into their language.
I plunge my hands in water,
and fill with sadness
from a place so far away
not even memory can travel there.

My daughter,
whose little history
contains two winters only,
doesn't see the shadow in the mirror,
that arrives by night, says, amazed,
'You're making a slide on your face'.
I smile for the first time.

On the street
the sun touches my ear, my shoulder,
like an old friend not needing conversation.
The boy beside me laughs.
He has seen the moon still hanging in the sky –
a half forgotten, half remembered face,
a lamp left burning overnight
for unexpected visitors.

Absence

At night the streets are rolled up,
and the houses stacked neatly away.

The wind walks down off the hill,
lifts the roof with one finger, to see if I am in.

Shadows shrug their tall shoulders.
Chairs shrink like spiders into dark corners.

Dogs look to rattled windows, alert as priests,
while pale dolls weep softly into their sheets.

The dead walk past deep in conversation.
They walk absently into sleep's open mouth.

By morning everything is back in place.
I step in a spillage of sunlight.
A blackbird flies singing from the water tap.

The Convenience of Bridges

1

We are full of bridges.
The bridge you see over your shoulder on a dark night
and can never find again. Nightmare bridge.
The beautiful white bridge in the middle of dream lake
nobody sets foot on.

The grandfather takes the child by the hand to the bridge.
But they never cross it. She never wonders why.
It is embedded. Look, that's where you have to go!

The old bridge upstream stretched as far as it could.
It took itself to the middle and stopped,
the unworked edge of stone still visible.
The bridge that takes you half way over.
and disappears under your feet.

He was doing so well, building as he walked.
Did he fall mid stream into the tidal water?
Or did he keep on walking, walking on air?

2

Something stopped the grandfather stepping onto the bridge.

People speak of death as the crossing of bridges.
The untroubled walk to the unknown country.
The crossing of t's and the dotting of i's.

We don't remember the days of the turbulent current,
unpacified pain, the fear of not paying the ferryman enough,
so he spits on his hands and rows out in the stream, cursing.

We take ourselves conveniently across bridges.

Death is the bridge swept away from under us.
Now, only now, you put your foot on it gingerly,
the parapet under your fingers. You make the first move.

In the Imperial War Museum

In a letter
handwriting sprawls, off duty, teeters
on the brink.
Ink fading into washed out sky. The weft
of paper lifted with neglect
and damp,
the regimental stamp. Folds opening
like lungs hinged to lost words.

Stink of fibreglass trench under the simulated
                 bluster of guns that thump
the underside of imaginary clouds.
Rag hair under a tin hat unnerves the touch.
Rats in plastic hiatus on the rim
like held breath composing platitudes
to dampen down the fear,
here and at home.
These fabricated reconstructions –
static as narrated dreams,
not the crawling, warm, wet pulp of nightmare.
Terror lashed down by tedium.

What we think, he doesn't talk about –
out there, waterlogged, mud encrusted, under
thunder clogged skies. Up
and over into metal rain. Horses
like plough teams struggling in flooded furrows.
What he knows about death
is nailed upside down to a fence, crow's wing
flapping in gusts,
slack necked, the crystallised eyes
like shattered ice.

Burst wounds of fading words scrawled across page
after page of ordinary details
that ambush our outrage. The real guns
are rusted, silent. These words
boom
and boom.

Arms

After the blast only the eye is calm.
I don't care who it was, I know it's done –
a rocket in a block of flats and one
man walking blind, his dead child in his arms.

A zealot's eye, the cold butt on the palm:
some finger pulled the trigger on the gun,
some boy, some man, some fucking mother's son.
This girl is any daughter; ours his arms.

In quiet pools of sexual regret
we never think that murder is the plan,
that we were born to do each other harm.
You'd think you'd see it once and not forget.
You couldn't wish it on another man –
the vacant eye, the empty, aching arms.

Removals

A man on the stairs glances over his shoulder,
holding a painting. It's the look spring gives to winter.
A woman in T-shirt and jeans fills the doorway.

There's a man with my name in the room stirring paint.
The walls wait blankly in smears of thin sunlight.
A desk lies dismantled on uncarpeted flooring,
its papers bagged in bin-liners, ready to go.

A girl stands at the window. Sunlight plaits her hair.
Thoughts spill like coloured beads over the sill.
Her brother, hair like corn, dawdles by the table.
Days trail him the way he leaves clothes where they fall.

The girl turns. The boy stares beyond her at the wall.
The woman, arms akimbo, distracted in the room's centre.
Front door open, they are carrying out the last picture.

Holiday

We took a walk every evening,
the light binding us in fine threads,
to look out to sea, the far, bright sea.
Father in new daps. Mother with coat wrapped round her,
me, 15, captive in chains of mother love.
We stood shivering in shop doorways eating chips,
before we turned in at the bed and breakfast.
Nothing was ever quite right for my mother,
my dad always trying to make it so.
We sat on a sweltering pebble beach
on plastic lilos with another family.
I wanted other eyes on me, other words.
The weather was wonderful, the sea, deep,
and we were only an hour from home.

Fear

Somewhere it crawled into me –
a rat in a pipe, so that,
when the children come in laughing
from the garden, I know
they will never come that way again.

A child myself by the makeshift hen house
of tea chests, roof felt and chicken wire,
I stood watching those fussy little women
come peck pecking towards me
in their drab, brown, puritan dresses
and blood soaked neckerchiefs.

Above me a grim face I call 'Father',
his hand like blue cheese on the axe handle.

The chickens are long dead,
their carcasses, half built cathedrals,
congealed on the kitchen table.
The hand is empty at father's side.
But still fear resides
in rooms of nervous, scratchy women,
who come at me with their beady eyes.

Or, dreaming in the dead of night, I fall
like a mason's mallet from a wooden tower
under the high leaf-fringed vaulting, leaving only
chiselled faces, stone eyeballs, uncompleted smiles.

Shells and Butterflies

She told him she was a student of optometrics,
as she walked him down the long corridor.
When they turned the corner, she put his hand
on her breast. Her nipple looked like a pink shell,
but it didn't feel like a shell at all.
Later he ran his hands down her belly –
butterfly wings on the thick shrub of hair.

He didn't know, whether to love her or collect her.
He took out his pin, inserted it deftly,
felt for the flesh, withdrew it, sucked the brine
through his teeth, careful not to spill a drop.

He took photographs of her body,
some close up, others from the edge of space,
her breast the shape of Columbus' world,
her wedge of hair an arrowhead flying towards him.

When they were developed, he put them away
in a drawer, forgot them. But sometimes,
deep inside him, a butterfly stirred, kicked
off her chrysalis and spread her wings over him.

When he died, someone went to see him,
and came back saying he looked like an empty shell.
But she knew where he was. She went looking for him
like a butterfly walking on a dried pool,
searching in the mud cracks with her proboscis,
sometimes opening and closing her wings,
shimmering her soft sea-shell colours.

Eurydice

I remember everything perfectly,
shaken out of the day's conciousness
like loose change from a dead man's pocket.
Last night I went down into sleep's subway,
half empty carriages rattling past.
You stood on the platform with your mother,
looking in my direction. I whistled for you.
You weren't listening. Your hair was corn stubble,
your breasts the burial chambers of anonymous kings.
I was the archaeologist of desire.

The train doors closed like a scallop shell.
Your blackbird mother called you back to her,
and pulled a veil of evening over your fields.

I jangled on into the sleeping suburbs,
where leaves curl like lips, sardonically,
at this ridiculous self I wear –
sliding on frozen oceans in dancing shoes,
the melody unravelling like a bandage.

Now, in the middle of a conversation,
a mouth is a crumpled skirt, or subway doors
opening and closing, far, far away,
saying, 'Speak to me!' When it is too late.

Hackenback's Limp

Let me tell you the story of Hackenback's limp.
He was wired up cruelly from ankle to knee
to God knows where, and he crawled on all fours,
or so Magda says. Can we go for a walk?
Oh, I'd love to, but Lulu is waiting
to show us her bike. It's years since I saw you.
I promised her mother. I wanted to ask you
about your affairs. I don't want to make love,
not try to recapture what wasn't there then.
What happened to you? Is Hackenback yours?
And how many children did you manage to have?
Are you still with that man? I hear him most nights.
He seems to know so much, everything,
I feel quite unable to cope. Do you think about me?
I went blind, but you know that. I wrote you a letter.
I imagine you send all your children to school.
Like the rest of your set, the coffee and the concerts,
the smart conversation, the conference seasons.
Is this envy or longing I feel? I can't tell.
And would we still speak the same language as then?
Let's go for a walk. The rest are asleep.
It's warm, and you're wearing a dress like the one
you had on on the day we put in at the islands.
The cliffs were hunched over like scribes at a desk.
Oil trailed on the water like manuscript drawings.
It was then that you mentioned the eyes of the poet.
We had travelled all night in the face of the moon.
The stars were alive. Your short hair was tousled.
Boats were put down. We clambered on board,
steadied by hands that reached up like beggars.
The wake of the water behind us was burning.
You've not led me before. I'm quite good on the rocks.
And I want you to tell me all that you've felt.

It's sunny and warm and Lulu can wait.
You can start, if you like, with
Hackenback's limp.

Nag's Head, Cape Hateras

There were three of us in the tent. I was
delirious. Stepping outside to piss,
the night wrapped me in mosquitoes. I was
a silk sheet covered in loose stitches.
The moon hung there – an unenamelled tooth.

Next day they took the inner tent for shade.
It was an oven on the beach. I cooked.
Deliriously I did handstands in the surf
to cool my head. I was a virgin sailor,
before he walked out, musket in hand,
across the Hateras swamps, claiming the land.

In the motel I drank eight pints of water,
and slept three days. They sat by the pool,
reading like strangers in an airport lounge.

Montana de Oro Bay

Where the headland cliff drops like a stone into the sea,
carved from black rock,
a solitary cloaked mourner, round shouldered in silhouette.
The dark, still presence disturbs its wings
like a broken umbrella. A cormorant
watching sea splintering over shelves of shale
along the cluttered shore line.

Now we hang like watery birds of prey
over our own slow moving, unsuspecting shadows.

Two hundred years ago holy intruders anchored here
in the bay. Hauling down swords and bibles.
They shaded their eyes against the climbing sun,
watched a gang of cormorants like poised pall bearers
on the rocks, examining disruptions in the depths.
They saw Chumash canoes ride the galloping waves
to meet them, weighed down with Abalone shells,
low in the water, while, far beyond them,
Californian Poppies turned the hills to gold.

Disney World

I dream of eating pink ice cream through keyholes,
bankrolls of notes that flicker like Victorian porn
on windy piers – What The Butler Failed To See.
I dream of lift shafts, holes in the ground,
water levels rising and men with grainy faces
staring sidelong at the camera.

In the daylight I ransack books of poems
for film names, production companies,
trailer blurbs and poster slogans.
My secretary brings me a coffee to my desk.
She sprawls across it, half undressed, her breasts
flattened on the shiny surface. Watching
the loose curl on her neck, I'm the King of the Jungle.
The air conditioning hums. The rubber plant droops.
I write in duplicate my expense account.

The Plan

You always had a plan. A plan for living in –
a job, a wife, a three-bedroomed house. Every time
you came home, you propped it up against the table lamp,
made small adjustments with a pencil stub,
checked your bank statements. Your wife grew big.
That was the plan. One night she didn't take the pill
and you were flying. Right up until the birth,
the birthing room and everything. Everything
was right – the scan, the baby-grow, the time.
You held her hand and heard the baby cry.
It cried and cried and never looked like stopping.

Now if you tease her, she screams. She's fourteen.
In all those years you had to find it out.
She's never planned a thing. Even the psychologist
was lost. They put her here because they didn't know
what else to do. She doesn't know how old she is.
She wanders round the room inspecting moments
and then dropping them. She's never held a pencil,
never made a plan, and never will.
You'll do it for her till your time is up.

Scrap

She's done the round of class, learned to assert
herself. Slogans come tumbling from her mouth.
Don't bother her with maps! She's heading out.
It's you have failed. You're scrap. You're obsolete.

She wants her friends to change. She's dyed her hair.
She'll sometimes nail you with her anecdotal youth,
and stub out failure under her bare feet.
Success demands a distance from the truth.

We wait with bated breath to hear whose fault
her life is next. Accept you're in retreat.
Her soup's gone cold. She's eyeing the dessert.

The Garden of Eden

You feel it crawling at your feet. The pressure drops.
The temperature that steadied once begins to bend.
The air is clammy at your throat. You hadn't noticed
layer on layer of meaning building up. Nobody told you.
Nobody was there, or so you thought. This summer idyll
coming to an end, before it had begun.
You were surprised by unleashed whispers, cool breezes
like a child's breath. And as for her enchantment,
it was the spell of childhood. Childhood, that is,
until she dropped her dress. You watched her hand up-arching
secretly in shadow, gloved in apple leaves.
The loosened breast. She looked at you.
You filled her eye. Her mouth was wet.

Ark of the Covenant

Think of the poor sods who carried the Ark of the Covenant.
They put it at the far end of the Temple
among the pomegranates, bulls and date-palms,
a place for God to live. Imagine,
standing all day in the presence of God, so close
you can hear him breathe. You carry this heavy thing
from place to place, wondering what it is
you are carrying. You feel it move,
adjust its position. Your knees buckle.
Your need for meaning heavy as a hollowed tree.
You carry it from place to place, because you have no choice.

Jacob's Ladder

First, there was the wrestle with the angel –
just like being in the womb with him again,
that delicious smell of love and danger,
up till the angel kicked me in the groin.

I grew smooth, cautious, planed along the grain,
avoiding knots, looking for the angle:
my first born brother innocent as rain,
headlong, God's fool, a cup without a handle.

After I did the dirty on my dad,
the flat, ungiving desert suited me.
The ladder in the clouds was all I had.
The hurricane of power uprooted me.

Lying, restless, on stones gives you a hard head.
I signed a contract with the Living God.

Holding On

We found my sister's grave sunk in the ground.
'3-in,' my father said, and he was right –
a man too old to reckon where he is
from day to day. A bleak and empty place.

The traffic climbed the long slow hill to town –
everybody going somewhere fast.
We straggled, almost nonchalant with expectation.
My mother walked ahead into the past.

The grave was there, cheap marble pulled apart,
as if the ground had trembled from the hurt.
I thought it was the wind caught in my coat –
my earth bound mother sobbing down the years.

Workmen had laid skewed slabs of concrete on the grave,
as if to keep her in, to keep her down.
She wasn't there. I stood imagining the bones.
My father walked away just like he always did.

My mother never saw him cry; but once
she caught him in the shed, head bowed,
his dirty hands, his shoulders shaking,
putting all my sister's books and clothes in order.

My mother said she saw her on the stairs,
and then she lived with us forever –
a happy, gentle, bookish girl of ten.
She must have thought that all of time was hers.

I watched my father rearrange the stones,
still strong enough to lift and drop and lift.
My mother put fresh flowers in the pot
– and so we left her.

Is this a life? Imagined ways of being,
a few old clothes, bones, and a ceaseless wind;
a girl remembered in a marble cage,
sorrow still kicking after all these years.

Cow

Mother, there's a cow in the front garden.
She's eating the Rowan tree,
and the postman won't come in.

A crowd is gathering in the street.
A police car is pulling up,
its blue light flashing.

Look, Mother, they are coming up the path,
a rope halter in their hands.
They're knocking at the front door.

They're asking me questions, Mother.
Who am I? What shall I say my name is?

Say 'Moo' dear, just say 'Moo'.

They're leading me away, a rope round my neck.
Somebody with soft hands is putting a hood over my head.

Can you still see the cow, dear? Can you still see the cow?

The Train

My father sits impassively and I, opposite,
mirroring his silence. The two women speak.
A spellbound tiredness wraps me in spider threads.
My mind the desert of a poem. Nothing to say.
My mother is struggling with a resolution she cannot find.
The years have drifted past, and now she can't remember,
or won't remember, who and what, and will not answer why.
Like passengers in a rail carriage
that no longer exists – the facing seats,
the leather window strap, the maps of England behind the heads,
watching a landscape washed in smoke and sunlight racing by.

There in the waterlogged meadow stands the girl.
The hedges hung with spiders' webs that flutter
like Tibetan prayer flags. Someone took a razor to the sky.
Alone, with her camera focused on the retreating train.

My father is silent, as he always is,
and soon the women fall silent too,
and I only say, 'It's time to go'.

A Dream of Football

Three ghosted men play football in a dream,
my mother's brothers and my Dad. One dead,
one rich – green Mercedes with a special plate,
and my 90 year old father, playing football
in the wooden slatted, green felted garage
of my boyhood. They are all my age now.
The garage as it was, timeless, falling down,
windows held in by rusty nails, putty cracked.
My dad, bow-legged like Stanley Matthews, shoots.
The ball and my uncle crash into the window,
a zig zag crack the length of it. They stand guiltily,
Giacometti figures in a concrete landscape.
They look like boys. They laugh. They have come alive.
They are and are not there. As if death was only a dream
or a memory. As if life was a dream. Three men my age,
all boyish fears, all happy in their manliness.
I watch them now, as I did then.
Unable to join in. Waiting my turn.

Dissolution

The body will fall somewhere. A dropped ice cream
out of a child's hand. A frozen estuary
to an invisible sea. Occasional wasps.
Colours leached out. What remains is a stain,
the slow erosion of recognition.

You think by asserting you take a hold,
but your throat swells up. Nobody listens.
The words get squeezed and never spoken.

You're here because they tell you you are something,
but nothing is graspable. Your children
are old enough to stay away from home.
You sleep in their beds secretly in the night,
imagine them asleep; you even dream their dreams,
while the silence in your throat is melting.

The Laugh

I watched the women and my mother
dressed in overalls and head scarves
folding sheets in half;
she gave me two corners and told me
just to stand there and hold them up;

all the women talking at once
about things I'd never heard of.
It was warm in the laundry,
and I was warmed by the women's secret hum.

Here it is again,
the women looking back at the painter,
in head scarves and aprons,
arms akimbo, laughing, open-mouthed,
squinting into the sun;

the women's voices I lived my childhood in,
my mother and her daughters, come back,
stitched with impudent laughter,
folded over me like warm sheets.

The Stranger

It was very cold and everybody talked about the War.
The stranger leaned the dining table on its side to stop the draught,
and chopped up furniture to keep the fire in.

I think he was a hunter. I was dressed in furs.
He put me on a sledge he made,
and carried me over the frozen canal.

Sometimes I caught him in bed with my mother,
but mostly he was out hunting.
He came home smelling of oily rags.
He came and went like a cat with a cat's meow.
He stayed even when we had all left home,
and when I came back, he always said, "Hello, Stranger".

Scrape

We always played close to the ground
in corrugated gutters
where glass eye marbles rolled and bounced skew-whiff
across gaping drains, level with dry dog shit.
We built our ramshackle shelters under bushes,
squatted like bushmen nose to nose with beetles.
Rats ran out as big as dogs.
We crawled and tasted dirt
under allotment gates. Occasionally
we clocked the light. It told us we were late
and heading for trouble. In the dusk our knees burned,
little beads of blood on the scraped skin.

Whenever we bumped into the big people,
our hearts stood still. They smelled of
boiled washing, baby-sick, swarfega and piston oil.
They spoke in hard looks,
that stopped us in our tracks, hands in pockets,
fingering marbles, dead fag ends, our growing selves.

Epithalamion

I stand ankle deep in shallow water
And fill my hand to wash away the blood.
It cools me down, but it isn't the river.

Once I picked oranges out of warm trees,
skins flaking under my fingernails.
A wild tortoise tottered the contours of my palm.
Laughing, we toppled him from hand to hand,
but I learned love in other, rougher gardens.

I remember your face close up to the mirror,
your big hand working scissors over beard and hair.
Then you were surrounded by colour.
I looked for that face again in the mirror today,
and saw only this face you have now,
clean-shaven, the mouth straight, the eye dull.
Over your shoulder was nothing, absolutely nothing.

Sometimes, when you're not looking, I swim
to an island in the river, my hands like fins.
The water opens up to them.
I am a turtle looking for a place to lay her eggs.
Once I found Gladioli there, tall as a man,
and black bear shit. But no bear.

I know there are people across the river.
Their smoke, like ghosts, rises at evening: and songs,
when the wind is in the right direction,
though the words die before they can reach me.

Here our children play games in the muddy water,
and throw their wet arms around my neck,
rubbing their little, smooth, wet faces against my bruised face.

At night you hold me down and look up,
up at the scudding clouds covering the grey moon.
Far off I hear the river. It is full and fast.
It tells me marriages go on for ever.

Happy Families

It came to me one dusk and licked my hand.
we lay awake all night – me and my new friend.

I listened for my father in the dark
And felt his magic fingers on my cheek.

Mother shivered in the window seat,
Living the grey rain on the blank street.

She wanted to go, but couldn't leave me.
She never asked about the wolf; she loved me.

At night I took dictation.
I found the ways to rhyme Boo-hoo and Howl.

Dad and I went once to see my Mum
where doctors surgically removed her dreams.

She had a look about her now we'd never seen.
The doors slammed shut. The corridors were green.

We rode in silence on the empty bus,
the street lights in the rain, the two of us.

My father screwed up poems to light the fire.
It was the time she used to call the quiet hour.

When she came home, she couldn't find her boy:
the wolf had swallowed him and gone away.

Self Portrait with House

I am wearing my house on my head
like a hat tipped over on one side
so that my curls are outbuildings tumbling down the hill.

Under my chin is my family
sheltering from the rain of thought
that might fall at any moment.

There's me, the two women and the child.
My hair has grown long like a girl's
and the black line of my shoulder takes up no room.

I am happy to be here drawing myself
in this manner, house, hat, shoulder
and family all making marks on me.

Sound

I put him out there in his pram
in the yard under the fig tree.
I was brushing crumbs off the table.
I heard the little sound like a bird,
an ooh like a dove under the fig tree.

My instinct kicked me outside
to check the cat wasn't sitting on him.
His face was a warm moon with thumbprints,
his mouth puckered up for the breast.

I saw the green fig leaf he saw
turn to gold in a breeze. I couldn't
wait to tell you. I leaned in
on him and kissed his wet mouth.

Now he rings on his mobile
and tells me about his walk
from lectures through the cemetery,
about the leaves on the trees
over the graves of dead children.

Nothing changes us at heart,
even though he can lift me now
in that crushing way men do.

We left the house, the yard where
the pram stood by the gate
that hung broken on its hinges.
It's now a couple's city flat.

All changed, but that sound of a dove,
that ooo
through the universe that sits there
under the fig tree waiting for us to hear it.

The Disappearance of the Sock

You used to see the two of them,
both brown, one on each ankle crossed.

They went together in the wash
among the school shirts and French knickers.

You watched them tumble round, so quick,
so loose, you thought there might be three.

Checking the empty dryer, there was one;
one or other – they didn't have a name – had gone.

You stand and run your fingers through your hair,
and think of other things that disappear,

half songs, a phrase, a name, a family word
gone, too, into another, other world.

Daughter

You call me up out of the blue,
out of the blue sky,
standing there in the frost,
watching your boyfriend play football.

You've walked up the hill, breathless
from a lecture on the psycho-pathology of children.
I interrupt. It's a mistake.
You have more to say.

You're laughing at your boyfriend
who just pushed a guy,
and the other side scored.
You speak to a passing boy.

When the game is over
I hear you say
Tom touched my bum,
and your boyfriend kick the ball away.

'Lay off my daughter's arse,'
I want to say,
'Lay off her mind'.
I want to say all that.

But stay silent,
knowing she is out there
in the sunshine and the frost
in the company of strangers.

Shaving the Fool

Fool, come here! Let me shave you.

Where are you?

I am here.

But I can't see you or feel you.

*No, that's right. Neither up nor down,
nor inside, nor outside.*

Who do you think you are?

*I don't know. I get bored.
The more I talk the more bored I become.*

What about silence? Why don't you try silence?

*Not possible. Not now.
As soon as you're born,
it starts up like a hire car driving across the desert.
It's a beautiful ride to begin with,
the empty road, the scrub and snakes and cactus trees
like men beseeching rain, but then
it goes on and on
for what seems a lifetime.*

Which, of course, it is.

*You turn on the air-conditioning,
tune in the radio to kill the voice,
but it won't stop. Even when you're asleep,
on and on, so you can't help asking,
when you wake up unshaved in some dirty motel room,
the sweat running over your body like a lizard,
Where are you? And the voice
can't help but answer, I am here, Fool,
let me shave you ...*

Tally

I watch you count your money on the step,
out loud, the cash your mother told you
not to lose. It doesn't add up.
You had to buy a wedding dress,
two children with all their cut-out clothes,
a house, a holiday, a Rowan tree
to keep out witches, painkillers
and a bottle of nightmare cure.

The street is empty and utterly silent.
Everybody is indoors dusting furniture,
with feathers or a torn up party frock,
I don't want you to cry,
but I can't find what you've lost, here,
between you, me and the gatepost.

Wardrobe

She was lying on rough stone with her long summer dress up
                  around her hips
and her hand between her thighs. I reached over the wall for her
and took her outstretched finger, her middle finger, full into
                  my mouth, releasing it
slowly to the tip. Her legs slumped open like *The Book of Kells*.
When her mother arrived, she pushed her dress down, and
                  I ducked behind
the crumbling wall, I lay still, breathless, like a hunted fox.

The girl was up on her long legs by now, beckoned me
with a toss of her hair into the great house. I went up
the wide staircase, looking for a bedroom with crisp sheets.
                  Everywhere was
clogged with sawn-off branches, garden trimmings. There was
                  washing piled up
along the landing and, looking over it, I caught a glimpse,
through the window, of the garden sundial, its shadow
                  striking twelve.

I heard the mother's voice and ducked into an oak wardrobe.
I nestled there, holding the velvet dresses next to my face;
veiled hats and shoes all shaped to feet. I breathed in the
                  smell of woman
that carried me wildly across the low hills of childhood,
looking in darker wardrobes. By the time she discovered me,
I had already landed like a parachutist swaddled in silk.

Winging It

I took the floor with heavenly people.
They were magnificent, my heroes.
There was Michael. When he stretched,
his nails scraped the ceiling.
He moved with such feeling
the room held its breath. I watched.
I tottered. I scored zeroes.
Michael asked me to make a couple.
He was tall and supple.
I was a ball. He was arrows.
He talked of love. I bitched.
He was the apple of God's eye. I was the peeling.
I was sick of pulling, hauling, toiling
in our father's yard, last hired, soonest ditched.
When my turn came, I always froze.
Not this time. Not now. A ripple
of applause swelled to a rush. I didn't topple.
I was winged. I was Icarus. I was Eros.
I was light as air, a kite, a bird. I blushed.
The polished floor below me filling
with amazement, men and women calling.
I wasn't them. I wasn't falling.

The Poet Reclining

I lie down in this wide,
warm air, in my purple shirt,
my straw hat beside me.
Across the field
a stable with a horse and foal
sniffing, and flicking the air.

Beyond the fields a line of woods
like a narrow moustache,
neat as my black shoes
I haven't taken off,
and beyond the moustache
the blind pink and blue face of the sky.

Under my eyelids anything
might come, so that on this journey
I have to lie down and rest
because I am a poet,
and the more I lie down,
the more I work.

This Poem

There are no doors and windows
in this poem.
It clings to the hillside
like a cloud about to rain,
roof open to the sky,
sparrows in the rafters.

There is no line
and no train of thought pulling words along
at twilight in dark wagons
that have left the station
but still haven't reached here.

I stand in the kitchen
of the poem that doesn't exist,
my heavy coat unbuttoned,
my scarf undone.

I stroke the cat
that pads with care across the void.
The kettle clicks.
I listen to the noisy silence
of scrabbling mice.

Guilty

His trial was held in the saucer of a cup.
The judge stirred the tea,
and twelve sugar lumps
concentrated on evidence
before melting into a verdict.

After the shouts from the gallery
he was hauled down into the biscuit barrel,
where he did solitary
for the rest of the afternoon.

When he got out,
the wife had left him for a Jaffa Cake.
Nothing was the same. A tea bag in a cup,
powdered milk, the radio on all day,
petty nibbling.

The Fiery Lake

The walk was as long as a sermon,
hot and blasphemous,
and the rocks we sit on burn our skin,

while the new couple
strip off their clothes,
and sploosh into the water.

They lie there on their backs
looking into the furnace
of the blaring sky.

We watch them squint-eyed
under the shade of our hands,
and then without eyes,

until they call, Come in, come in!
We pretend not to want to,
and begin the walk home

along the pastures of purgatory,
by the river of neglect,

hours and hours of the same feeling
under our hats
and in our clenched fists.

The Rule

The rule is you get up earlier than you would like.
Your heaviness makes each stair creak.
You step in the warm spot the dog has slept on.
The rule is he gets up slowly out of your way.
The rule is you stand naked in the kitchen
and try to remember what it is you do next.
The low tide of anxiety pours in
over the pleated sand bed of your heart.

You try a walk in the park.
The rule is you don't talk to anybody.
Somebody asks if you're alright. You say,
a fly has landed in your eye. You stop.
The trees in the park are blurred with summer.

Straw Hats and Parasols

I am in the familiar room
that smells of wood
and warmed up dust,

and the children
have run into the playroom
to put on boas
and floppy hats,
the boy in a tight little brown dress,

the two of them will trot out
with wicker prams and armfuls
of rag dolls to be named
ceremoniously by me on this dining chair.

Something pulls at my elbow;
it is only time
circulating
like water over a weir.

Their mother comes into the room
carrying hot plates in outstretched hands
from oven to table top.

She doesn't see me.
I sit absolutely
still on the dining chair.

She doesn't see me; she sees through me
as if I am absence.

Hedda Gabler

After the gun went off, she vanished.
I looked at the empty seat.
The blast had spread a silver light
over the first few rows.

I imagined I'd been shot,
and wondered what the hole in my shirt looked like,
the startled hands, the wind tunnel face:
what a mess the sudden ends of evenings make.

She was on the pavement, hailing a cab;
back there two sad people dead in the wings.
I thought I heard Ibsen's scratchy nib
Rewrite the final lines.

So I was willing to throw my body
into the back of the taxi;
her wet eyelashes, her open coat,
I could hardly hold my wallet steady.

What to Do?

Two people silent in a room:
he isn't looking. She cries into her hands.

Once he stood here in the doorway,
while two jackdaws flew from the fireplace
round and round the room.

They dipped through the open window
across the lawn, under the witch hazel
and down the dreaming, spring-warm, vacant street.

She is staring at the face she left in her hands.
The window is wide open.
He sees time rush through her hair like wind.

The Poet in the Rain

The rain is falling on the corrugated cover of the chicken shed.
It's rattling the metal roof and the earth is churning.
I am dragging the goat from behind a big cloud.
All the doors and windows of the barn are open.
Eyes watch me from the dry straw.

The goat has stiffened his legs.
He isn't budging. I am pulling on the rope around his neck.
And the rain is falling in stair rods
onto the dirt that is churning over in mud,
where the chickens are squawking
and lifting their wet feathers off the ground.

Oh, it is raining. It is raining,
but I am as wet now as I will ever be,
The ground as muddy, the chickens as bedraggled as they will ever be,
and the goat,
stiff-legged and grunting,
will always be outside in the rain
with me and my aching arms eternally.

Wash, O God, Our Sons and Daughters

He watches from the lit window of the Lake Hotel.
He is wondering where life is. He knows,
even in the warm room, he isn't safe.
He looks for his sister's hand: it isn't there.

Stars shine in the liquid mirror of the lake,
and in the dark a woman swims voluptuously
like his sister rising in the arms of the preacher
from the waters of purification.

Supper is laid for one in the dining room
under the candelabra and the stag's head.
He stares at the empty suit of armour
in the fireplace, and walks out

across the lawns to the lake, which is so black
he keeps on walking over its oily surface,
bending to pick up the stars one by one
and put them in his mouth. They are brittle sparks.

He can hear the plock and scuttle in the reeds
on the far bank, the plangent crawl of the woman
swimming away from him. He hears, as he sinks,
the thin music of baptismal hymns.

Man with a Suitcase

The man bending over the suitcase
His long coat covering his boots,
could be the back end of a pantomime horse.

He may never get up again.
He may grow old this way,
curved over like a flower wanting rain.

If he picks up the suitcase, the lid
will fall open; his inward life
spill out like a burst wound,

If he takes his belt off to bind it,
his trousers will fall down round his ankles;
he will be a child paddling in shallow water.

So he leaves it there, leaves off the struggle
and stands up straight;
he is a young man again with a red face.

House Hunting

Upstairs on twisted landings in an evening light
we listen. Each room below inhabited
by shut pianos and pianissimos
like narrow lips on angry silences,

the window frames ill-fitting, rain in the cracks
are gathered tears, the garden's weed trimmed lawns,
its crumbling outhouses full of empty bottles
stacked next to mirrors cracked like drunken jokes.

Each must have thought this silence safe as houses,
when the rain poured down, before the kitchenware
was flying to the rafters in a rainbow arc
of knives and forks and fancy crockery.

The penny drops between the landing
and the master bedroom emptied
of double beds and other human kindness,
no wedding photographs, no family groups
on holiday in blinking sunlight.

In the doorway of a children's room
the agent sniffs and points towards a cage:
we peer and lean and glimpse, amazed,
a ferret snarling, crying for its master.

The Solid Body

That nothing is as it should be
is the hollow heart of everything we know.
Out of this flows
palpitating, living flesh
that will find its way as ash
into the blackened, leaf-mould earth
like a badger coming home for death.

You hold all the physicality I can muster,
loving the touch of other skin
the weight of breast, my finger on your spine,
non-existent as my own;
I know profoundly it is just air,
yet present in the way nothing else matters.
We listen to the mermaid's voice
calling us to this wind-swept grassy place,
so that this air at least will not forget us.

Return

I stand in your front garden
in the snow. It is snowing.
My footsteps have followed me.

Evening comes in a blue light,
blocks of yellow cut
from the window frames.

I stand like a Hazel tree
accumulating misgivings.

In the morning the door opens.
It's you who look out.
I wish I were a blackbird

in leafy summer with
delicate arpeggios.
But I am tongue-tied.

You close the door.
It doesn't dispel me.
Next year I come again.

I am not vexed
by your ignorance of me.
Even when I summon up

the courage to make a noise,
you say: Is somebody out there?
– and close the door.

There are wounds that do not heal
with time. They hurt again
in certain weathers.

The Iceman

All of me shrunk
to a crystal in the brain.
Nothing remains,
the bark of my skin
like frosted glass
on a black carcass.
The copper of my axe
is warmer, softer
than my heart after
the lingering romance
of dying or the dance
of the veils of mist
that locked as they kissed
the face exposed.
My mouth was glazed.
A grim determination
in my cracked eyes,
the blind horizon.
You can see now I wouldn't make it.
Take my temperature, take it.
Cut my tight sinews,
straighten my hands, you
who are remaking me
5000 years
after the tears
jewelling my eyeballs,
and the stumble and the fall,
the lying in state
without fire, without flute,
as snow fell, and the lies
layered up in ice
that you unpack
to a mystery, a trick.
I was crying to get home.
I was hurrying to build Rome.

Self Portrait with Saxon Helmet

The scissors skip and click like little birds
around my head,
the slender thumb and fingers at my ears weigh down each side
for symmetry.

In the depthless, pointless mirror I'm helmeted
like a Saxon lord,
pursued by hawks,
wings splayed in filigree across my nose, claws spread
for killing.
The eyes stare out with age-old cruelties and hunt me
to extinction.

The empty face looks back into a consciousness
of small vanities.
The woman puckering up my hair alerts me to a map
of grieving rivers
that trail their frozen histories across a landscape
where Saxon lords
are buckling up their horses for the ride,
the way we hunt
with squinting eyes for tracks of memory.

Nothing remains, of course, of melted flesh but golden
shoulder clasps
a silver bowl, Apostle spoons, this garnet studded helmet,
and nothing will remain
of us, no skin, no bone, no light reflecting eye,
no tender name,
no plumed breathed prayer to feather the air
with question marks
over the word-locked coffins of laconic warriors.

Winter Rain

You who are also water
rise to the moon's kiss
inside an imagined shell.

Everything is drummed
under the rain's percussion,
the leaf, the roof, the ground.

When it stops suddenly in the dark,
the silence slides into you
unexpectedly.

You look up and listen;
you can hardly wait
for the shell to burst,

and your watery voice
to leach quietly
over the sodden fields.

Anatomy of a Winter Evening

Sometimes, when the owls in the orchard hoot
in their rapture, I think I can hear
the mind ringing. It might be the blood
pulsing round the tiny veins of the inner ear.

Whatever it is, it stops me in my tracks
until the owl is silent,
and the bones of the ear settle to rest.

I am told, if you stand by the woodshed,
you can hear them.
I go to the woodshed and listen.

Nothing. One day
it will be the last day for standing
in the ringing cold,
the last cup, the last mouthful.

How, on a night like this,
can you be closer to anything
than that owl that hasn't called
on that tree that ceases to exist

out there in the darkness?

Snail

After the rain, the drench of sleep,
he trundles on, aloof,
a little potentate,

reading with that single hand
the surface grain
of soil and gravel

and deeper still
the low vibration of the inner coil
of earth.

If something shakes the land
he hides inside the helix,
eyes withdrawn, the life suspended.

Crossing shipping lines
in fog, he moves in hope
of grassy continents.

If we could walk as slowly,
and roll with that receptiveness,
we would feel moonlight crawl across our skin.

Rapunzel

I want to put my ear
on your still warm pillow
and listen to your dreams.
You say it is whimsical.

There's a fox stole nuzzling its snout
into the fold of the chaise longue
like a small child hiding
in her mother's armpit.

I want to sit on your winged chair,
my arms along your arms,
my back behind your back.
You say it is impossible.

I want to put my foot
on your neck. You say
it is an image of fascism.

The child lets out a laugh
that flaps and flutters
into the startled corners of the room.

You want to tie me to you
with your hair. I say
it is too binding.
You tell me I lack conviction.

You ask if I am interested in anything.
I'm interested in everything, I say,
but nothing in particular.

So we stand there in Wellington boots,
ashes in the grate,
the door jammed open on its hinges,
and watch pigeons flock through the broken windows
of the heart.

The Plunge

She had a button hanging from her coat
below her breasts. I wanted to resew it,
back under her breasts that pushed at the closure
of her outdoor woollen coat. But I didn't.
I spent the time watching it.
It wobbled like a dead flower on its stem.
What I said I don't remember,
but, when I spoke to her, I looked her in the eye.
It was Lake Tahoe
with two cowboys preserved entirely
by the cold in that immeasurable depth.
When she spoke, I could watch her teeth,
a stockade of brilliant white
that repelled savages. This way
I could keep an eye on the button that threatened
a catastrophic tumble
down the long front of her coat
that opened at the knee. She told me
about a class she was taking
in Ancient Civilisations.
Desire dribbled from me
like brain from a mummified Pharaoh.
My attention wavered. That was all it took
for the button to begin its drift downwards
like the first leaf in the New England fall.

Man in a Box

He was lying in a box, so beautiful,
though he wasn't my type.
I asked him the question point blank,
did you do it or didn't you?
Whether I did or whether I didn't, he said,
is neither here nor there.

Was he glad he had done it?
He didn't know it had happened.
He was sleeping, and the carpenter
used a rubber hammer.

I swear to God, he really didn't know
he was the most beautiful man
who had ever drawn breath. I kissed him
on his closed eyelids. His wet lashes
tickled my lips. Though I knew
he really wasn't my type, still
I climbed in and lay down with him
there in the box.

The Wish

If I could only
lower myself
gently like a bucket
in a well, down
into damp darkness
with the tinkle of
falling masonry
chasing me into
the murky water.
At the bottom, I would
put my hand in
and find another hand
I didn't know, but
it would grasp mine thinly,
and I would feel
for a moment satisfied,
a second, that is,
until I pulled back
and nothing came out
but my own hand.

Uses of a Goatherd

I read about a Mongolian goatherd
seven foot nine he was, with eleven inch hands.
How small the goats must look from that great height,
how soft the tiny teats on those rough fingers.

Trapped in a gathering of noisy people
I stare into a gin and tonic all evening.
I'd introduce him now and watch them
blench at his huge hand around the glass.

I imagine the snowy wastes, his hand-made boots,
him singing to himself deep in his throat.
Hurt and anger melt from me
like snow on a sleeve by the open stove.

I think of me and him meeting, not here,
the doors are too small, but in some wind-swept Yurt.
We would smile, and drink from the same cup:
I would lose my hand in his enormous hand
and my loneliness in his loneliness.

Midwinter

The owls are calling at the edge of darkness,
so we lock up the doors,
pull down the blinds,
and light a fire
to set the darkness free.

When I look up, you are sitting
in the room in a low light, reading.
Papers are strewn around the floor,
books open on your lap.

Who are you? Who lit the fire?
Who imagined the world into light?
And who is now covering the fields with darkness?

Love Poem

It's not your body
I want. It's more.
Something without a taste,
without a sound. And if
you can't or won't,
I'll stand and howl
all night outside your door.

Something defines you.
It's not your silky hair,
grey eyes, your smiling mouth,
nor yet your voice
that takes me south
far from my core.

When we come nose to nose,
forehead to head,
when we have our bodies
rise with the dead,
when you feel my hand
smooth out your back
like a map of noise,

then you must know
it's not your silly body
or your hair,
your serious face
or your despair,
that fills me with you
like the hedge with snow.

The Unexpected

We can never really know
what happens
before it starts,
if the clapping
will alarm us
out of the long
dreamy narrative
to be choreographed through,
all stage fright gone.

This time you
are funny, charming,
have us eat
out of your hand,
the sticky fundamentals
of your life
absorbed by evening dress
in the orchard's dappled light
at the outdoor supper
of Traviata.

Sooner than you think,
can think,
the blink of an eye,
time for the universe
to come to being;
time it takes
the burst balloon
to startle tears
is time enough
for you to feel a twinge
in an unexpected part
where you think
the liver is, the heart:

and sooner still
you're lying,
skinny on a bed,
not moving,
thinking
that the world can never end,

and in a way
it never does:
you take it with you –
apple trees, sky, Violetta.

Widow

She is being reborn, she says,
after all these years.
She doesn't want to be.
It's like learning to walk:
you keep being put down,
when you want to cling on.

I'm soaking prawns at the sink;
I lay their naked bodies out
to dry on kitchen roll.

It's like that, I think,
taking the mayonnaise from the fridge;
how grief flays us
and leaves us stumbling about
in a life that doesn't want us.

Indian Summer

A day of summer comes in September
unexpectedly like your accountant
bearing his soul. He's practising for the priesthood.

The guide dog stops to talk with an old woman
who asks him how his master is getting on.
His master sighs and sits down beside them
on the pavement, waiting patiently with doleful eyes.

Wood smoke drifts across the roof of the bakery
dragging with it the warm smell of new bread
and the background radiation of anxiety
that the fire will go out, that tomorrow
winter will bring rain and people wrapped up in coats
squabbling over which car they will ride to the funeral in.

Heart

Did it watch there on top of the world,
till its weight tipped forward on unfurled wings
rising and falling
like rain sweeping the valley sides?

What was not imagined dropped
out of the sky, snatched you,
lips cracked with cold,
fingers drawn up like talons.

Poor heart, what threw you unannounced
into this wrestle of feather and flesh?
Nothing prepared you
and nothing prepares you now.

In the beginning death prodded you along
from one ambiguous happiness to another.
Now it plucks and pulls at the entrails of your life,
till you go limp in the beak's dark appetite,

a question gasping out of you.

A Rainy Day

There's my neighbour already up,
chopping wet kindling for the evening fire.
We don't speak. He only waves
with one thumb in the air.
Worried about train times and taxis,
I forget him immediately.

The rain slants on the carriage window.
A tractor struggles in mud.
Somewhere we pass a white horse
standing in water, head
down, listening.

I come home in the dark.
There is a silence outside
I had never heard before
like a thought not expressed.
The newspaper is still folded
in his front door letter box.

There is a strange car
in the place he never parks
and a woman approaching
with a handkerchief
and a wild stare.

Against Time

Flick the coin off your fingers secretly
and let me find it by the roadside,
all of us in new pumps bought for the holiday.
Let me run back to you, coin in one tight fist,
and you be amazed in my amazement,
that warm, damp, dark evening on the Welsh road,
the last bus gone, and with your strong arms
lift me high on your shoulders like the victor from the field.

I am weaker now and more fearful,
and you, father, restored in dreams,
are not of the substance to raise me up
on your shoulders for one last time.

Dialysis

The wings I flew on all night are crumpled.
Dream fluid leaks from me. I weigh my shadow
to see if I have gained or lost. I take my seat
in a room full of whispering nurses.
My blood is running round the room on rails like a toy train.
I am a pale ghost pointing a finger.
The only language spoken is a pump pressure
and the ragged mathematics of a fever.

They push the blood back into me to kick-start my day.
I fly light-headed with the wound in my neck
over my bloodless shadow. Pulses drum in my ears.
I am flying through purgatory, burning off
the clatter of conversation.
It all falls away behind me like a comet tail.
I can't tell if it's the scream of receding earth I hear
or the woman of the camellias singing her heart out.

The Resurrection of the Body

Will it be like waking from an old sleep
on a train across the night-filled tundra
towards the Holy City, a sleep broken
by a loud rattling of chains, the warm dream-filled flesh
falling away over the high blue world?

Will the first thing you see be the last thing you saw?
Will the brightness of undiminished faces
blind you? They are not who you think they were.

Will your first gesture be a hand over the coffin's edge
like a languid arm dangling out of a summer canoe?
Will there be naked men lying tangled
like drowned swimmers in the grass,
their hair embroidered with forget-me-nots?

Will the dead soldier with apiary's eyes
lean on one elbow, check his wallet pocket,
get unsteadily to his booted feet, look around,
as if he has just remembered something, and leave?

The End

At some point
I will be watching from the cliff.
Yes, and you will gather round my bed
after the diagnosis,
and I will be trying to say
something meaningful to you all,

something that signifies a completion,
but you won't be able to read me
for the tears,
thinking of what to say
at the funeral – nothing too truthful,
nothing too wrapped in clichés,
and what to say to the little ones
when they ask.

Time will come closer
and closer to me,
up the bedclothes, across the counterpane,
into my breathing tubes,
and I will be the diver on the cliff,
balanced and still,
everything together in one breath,
the final revelation in a rush of air,

and you will all sit there
astounded by the feeling
I am no longer in this body,
and you will begin to make sense
of the situation you find yourselves in
without me.